TORONTO
The Celebration

By Rudi Christl and David Crombie

Aura One Enterprises Incorporated

Christl, Rudi, 1946-
Toronto The Celebration

ISBN 0-9684871-0-6

1. Toronto (Ont.) – Pictorial works. I. Crombie, David,
1936-
II. Title.

FC3097.37.C47 1999   971.3'54104'0222   C99-900794-7
F1059.5.T684.C47 1999

Aura One Enterprises Incorporated.
auraone@interlog.com

Design & Typography: Bruce Graham

Printed and bound in Canada.

Acknowledgements

I wish to thank
my sponsors for their generous support –
Leica Camera Division Kinderman (Canada) Inc.,,
and Photomethods Custom Colour Labs Limited.

I would also like to thank Mayor Mel Lastman
and Ed Mirvish for their contributions.
My gratitude also goes out to Tom McDonnell for
his invaluable assistance, Bruce Graham, Eva Hecht,
Pam Harrison and Michael Assaly for their
considerable time and effort on this project.
And finally, thanks to the human subjects of my
photographs, who were unwitting participants
in this book.

-R.C.

Some portions of the text have been previously published.

For Eva, Adam and Simon

CONTENTS

Foreword by Ed Mirvish

When I first came to this city at the age of 9 some 76 years ago, Toronto was a nice city of homes and churches but not much else. Back then, we had what were called "Blue Laws" (remember "Toronto the Good") – meaning that you could not buy anything, not even a bottle of milk, on Sundays. If you were caught doing business on our day of rest (and I confess I was caught more than a few times delivering groceries from our store on Dundas Street to our neighbours), the police would hand you a summons and you'd have to tell your story to the judge. It was a nice city but a dull one.

At the age of 26 I got married, and with the help of my wife's insurance policy (a grand sum of $214), we opened the store on Bloor and Bathurst Street which I guess everyone now knows as "Honest Ed's". As our business grew, so did Toronto. Probably the biggest changes started after the Second World War when so many immigrants came to Canada, bringing with them the vitality of many mixed cultures. In part thanks to all the newcomers, Honest Ed's continued to prosper. So when the city threatened to tear down the Royal Alexandra Theatre in 1962, I had the opportunity to buy it – not out of a major interest in theatre at the time, but because at $215,000 the Royal Alex was a great bargain (like everyone else who comes to Honest Ed's, I love a good bargain)! It's hard to imagine the Theatre District as once being desolate, given what it looks like today. But 37 years ago, there was nothing around the Royal Alex except railway tracks and freight sheds. To attract more people to the area, I decided to build a restaurant next door the theatre and I now have a string of them right beside the Royal Alex which people seem to enjoy. Part of the deal I made when I bought the theatre was that I had 5 years to make it work. At the end of those five years (and about half-a-million dollars later which was spent on restoration), we were breaking even and by that time I'd developed a real affection for the theatre. Since then our son David and I bought (and sold) the Old Vic Theatre in London, England which we owned for 16 years, and we built the Princess of Wales Theatre. Originally I never really wanted to be part of the theatre business or the restaurant business, but over the years I have developed an affection for both. I now am privileged and enjoy our theatres and restaurants.

In fact I feel privileged to be part of a country that gives people like me who had little formal education and no money, an opportunity to improve themselves. There are so many countries in the world where you can't get ahead no matter how hard you try. I'm still at the store every morning between 8 a.m. and noon, after which I'm usually at the restaurants and then in the production offices until the end of the day. Besides attending the opening night of our own productions, we also travel to openings of shows in other countries. But I'm always happy to come home. I think people who visit us love Toronto maybe as we do because it has all the big-city kind of things they like to do, but it's also safer and cleaner than many other large cities in the world. I myself enjoy walking through ethnic neighbourhoods like Chinatown and Kensington Market – I find them very interesting. Of course I enjoy Mirvish Village too. In the late sixties I bought up a whole block of Markham Street, just behind my store. It became an internationally famous area known for its art galleries, craft studios, bookshops and antique stores. The city declared it an Artist's Colony in the early seventies.

I think Toronto is an exciting city with so many nationalities and cultures here all mixed together. With our beautiful parks and recreation areas like the Toronto Islands, Harbourfront and all of the waterfront area including Ontario Place, I think the city is ideally situated. We are also a very important entertainment area, ranking third in the world. I've seen Toronto grow from no more than half-a-million people some 75 years ago, to almost two-and-a-half million today. Considering how the city has changed over those years, I have a lot of faith in Toronto and I'm very optimistic that it will continue to flourish.

I invite Torontonians and visitors to enjoy what Toronto has become: a diversified city, a big multi-cultural city, a residential city with green spaces everywhere you look. In short, Toronto is a city worth celebrating!

Ed Mirvish

Ed Mirvish

A Message from Toronto Mayor Mel Lastman

The Millennium.

It is a word that conjures a lot of emotions and a lot of images. The year 2000 is more than a milestone. It is a time to look ahead in wonder and in trepidation. It offers challenge and opportunity tempered with concern that we have to do it right – especially when considering a city of 2.3 million inhabitants.

I am more optimistic that we will do it right. I know we will use the challenge of a new millennium to make the greatest city in the world even greater.

We have the people, the wonderful quality of life, the will and the way. We are one of the most civilized and dignified cities of the world. We have an incredible new spirit to match our new amalgamated status.

We have achieved many successes since the new Toronto was born January 2, 1998, and I am confident we will build on that very short history and conquer the millennium with pride and distinction.

We have much to offer and much to give. Our city is now the fifth largest in North America. It is the most culturally diverse city in the world with people from 169 lands speaking over 100 languages.

We are the largest city in our country of Canada. We are the financial centre of our country. Socially, we are a microcosm of our country with a quality of life second to none.

In our short life, we have received world acclaim. The new Toronto is being viewed around the planet as a city that combines everything a big city should offer with the small town grace and quality of life that our citizens deserve.

Improving that model may sound difficult, but a great city is a city that constantly evolves, a city that constantly recognizes new challenges, a city that takes something inherently good and makes it better.

That's the future of Toronto as we grow together. We will make things better for our children's children.

The new millennium is not a finishing point. It's a starting point.

Mel Lastman

Mel Lastman

TORONTO – THE CELEBRATION

TORONTO – THE CELEBRATION

TORONTO – THE CELEBRATION

TORONTO – THE CELEBRATION

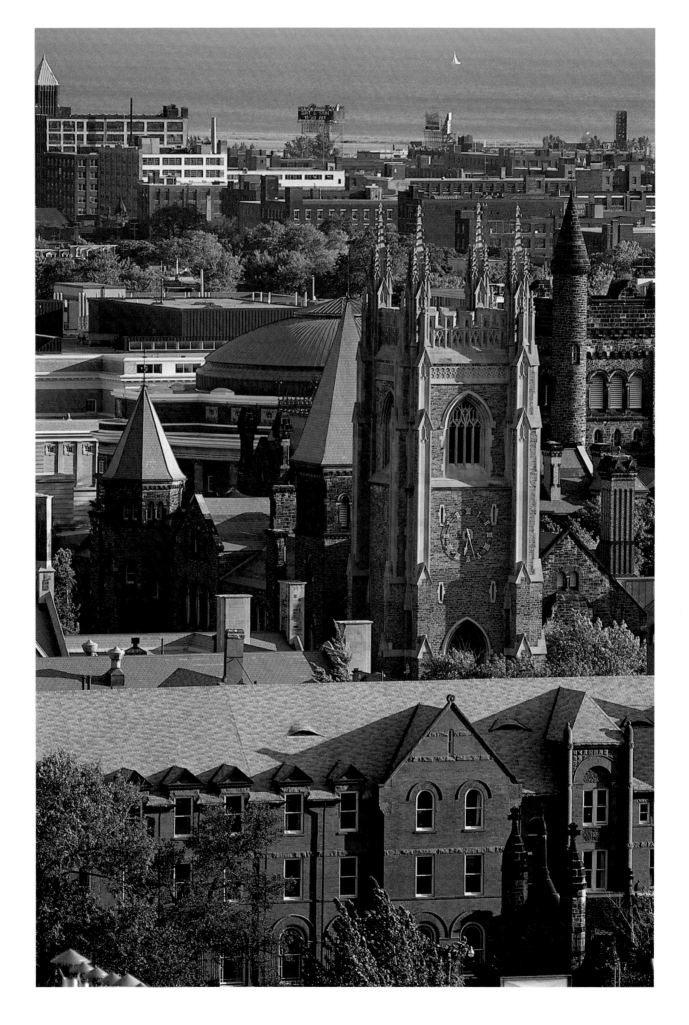

TORONTO – THE CELEBRATION

TORONTO – THE CELEBRATION

TORONTO – THE CELEBRATION

TORONTO – THE CELEBRATION

TORONTO – THE CELEBRATION

A GATHERING PLACE

A few years ago, when it was reported that the United Nations had referred to Toronto as the "world's most multicultural city," Torontonians were delighted but not surprised.

For decades, Toronto has been at the centre of a world-wide movement of people: from continent to continent, country to country, and country to city.

For more than fifty years, Toronto has annually become home to more than seventy thousand people from all over the world. Today, nearly half of all Torontonians were born in other lands. This extraordinary ingathering has transformed the demographics of the Toronto region. It has also brought with it the challenge of living in close quarters and shared geographic space, with diverse races, languages, cultures and religions.

"Toronto has always been a gathering place. In fact, its name comes from an aboriginal word expressing that concept."

Toronto has always been a gathering place. In fact, its name comes from an aboriginal word expressing that concept. Long before contact with Europeans, the Ojibwa, the Mississauga, the Iroquois nations and others came to Toronto, at the edge of the Pays d'en Haut (the "high country") leading to the upper lakes and the interior of North America. (This history was remembered during colonial days, when the province was named Upper Canada.) Here they established settlements, hunting grounds, and sacred places.

Later, the Europeans, mainly French and English, in pursuit of furs, converts, and empires, came to trade, to build forts and, ultimately, to settle. In the 19th and early 20th centuries, Toronto became a destination for many immigrants, mostly – but not exclusively – British.

In *Gathering Place: Peoples and Neighbourhoods of Toronto, 1834-1945*,
Robert Harney points out that this immigrant settlement foreshadowed
the "ethnocultures and ethnic enclaves in the city" following the Second
World War. For, despite a superficial ethnic homogeneity, these English, Irish,
Scots and Welsh immigrants were intent on expressing their separate
identities: faith, ethnicity, culture, lifestyle, and social organizations. Thus,
Toronto's "multiculturalism" was not born after the Second World War but
established by Anglo-Celt immigrants at least 150 years earlier.

The Canadian view of multiculturalism is rooted in its own history, and
differs from that of the United States. Arthur Schlesinger, Jr., in *The
Disuniting of America*, described the American attitude to achieving unity in
a multi-ethnic society as "the creation of a brand new national identity,
carried forward by individuals who, in forsaking old loyalties and joining to
make new lives, melted away ethnic differences."

Schlesinger accuses Canada of courting schism because, he says, "as
Canadians freely admit, their country lacks such a unique nationality." This
is an unfortunate misreading, of both Canadians and Canadian history, for
life holds more possibilities than merely segregation or assimilation. Indeed,
Canadian experience clearly shows a third way, which has been called
"cohabitation." The strength of "cohabitation" is that it implies neither
ignoring nor embracing those different from ourselves; it means simply
learning to dwell peacefully with them.

In Canadian cities, cohabitation was a fact of history long before multiculturalism became the subject of government policies. Our civic instincts
and traditions came from our involvement with the purposes and practices
of the Empire. Through participation in the British Empire, particularly,
Canadians grew accustomed to belonging to a global community of many
nations, languages, cultures, religions, and races. We identified with those other

splashes of British pink on the map: we were all British subjects, resident in our particular place but united by our allegiance to the Crown.

To be sure, there was hierarchy, racism, classism, colonial struggles and wars of Empire; but participation in the Empire enabled us to feel that we were a part of people and events beyond our borders.

Our Constitutional heritage, which supported and reflected our practical experience, insisted that language, culture, and community were local and place-related, even though we had significant – even supreme – loyalties beyond our borders. We had to be a political house of many mansions, in which there was room for multiple loyalties and acceptance of individual and community differences.

"On a planet of finite size, the most desirable of all characteristics is the ability to cohabit with persons of differing backgrounds and to benefit from the opportunities which this offers."

Canadians were not, however, striving to be mere celebrants of unrelated particularisms. We have always understood that our divisions needed to be rooted in common ground and that the price of continuing diversity is the endless search for unity.

As former Prime Minister and author of the Charter of Rights and Freedoms, Pierre Trudeau expressed it, "On a planet of finite size, the most desirable of all characteristics is the ability to cohabit with persons of differing backgrounds and to benefit from the opportunities which this offers."

This powerful message endowed the idea of the Canadian "mosaic" with a compelling sense of purpose, and extended the legitimate limits of diversity. It welcomed the distinctiveness of newcomers and minorities and provided them with a sense of belonging.

Whatever the consequences for national unity, this approach emphasized and legitimized our inclination for the global, the regional, and the local, and allows immigrant ethnic and racial communities to merge into Canadian society with a minimum of tension and violence. People are able to pursue old cultures, develop new identities, and participate in the general society at their own pace.

"The neighbourhood, with its familiar streets and institutions... becomes the 'base camp' from which newcomers can make sorties to pursue their dreams"

In Toronto, the experience of cohabitation takes place in our neighbourhoods and communities. These distinctive settlements allow for a sense of kinship, in places where particular customs, habits, and languages can be expressed, and the warmth of familiarity experienced. There work can be found, housing and transportation are cheap and convenient. They are dependable islands of human contact, offering coherence, predictability, and a web of helpful relationships to combat an often alien and sometimes hostile world.

Robert Harney describes such neighbourhoods as places that become the home, the yard, the marketplace, the town square, the social club, the defensible turf, and the playground. Here people exchange gossip, fight for points of view, meet and mate, organize social events, make personal decisions, and share collected wisdom. The neighbourhood, with its familiar streets and institutions – the settlement house, the school, the café, the corner store, the places of worship and recreation – becomes the "base camp" from which newcomers can make sorties to pursue their dreams. In doing so, Harney explains, they learn to "negotiate their ethnicity, and make those constant adjustments of style and thinking which are milestones in the process of learning to live within the larger North American setting."

Through this process, newcomers devise their own internal, biographic maps of the city: where home and friends can be found, where danger lurks, and where there are places to be avoided. These maps contain practical points of information about daily routines and social and sporting events. They also locate other places and people: an uncle in Chicago, a cousin "up north," places where work could be found, places where "they" won't hire. These maps represent the newcomers' sense of space, linking them physically and psychically to the things that are important to their known world and their future.

"Landmarks," a poem by George Jonas, who came from Hungary to make his own contribution to the city, describes his biographic map of Toronto:

> After sixteen years, I remember you
> Ossington bus, O'Leary Avenue
> Perhaps gravity makes them loom so large
> West Lodge, St. George Street, York garage.
> Northcliffe backyard, where cops used to appear
> after midnight to confiscate my beer
> or Glenholme boarding house, five bucks a room,
> whose dome languidly crumpled into doom
> and bursting water pipes had drowned on steam
> the ex-mate of a German submarine.
> The beanery on Queen Street where a lame
> girl first sat in my booth and asked my name.
> Or long before, a metal winter night,
> a funeral home's sign casting a light
> flickering blue on grey December slush:
> with cardboard trunks, torn clothes, needing a wash,
> an evil-smelling strange boy, tall and thin,
> had asked to spend the night. And God knows why
> they took me in.

Such maps are not static: they evolve according to what is known, what is learned, and what is dreamed. In short, they are keys to individual and group survival.

Newcomers, then, are neither fighting a rearguard action to preserve the ways of the Old Country culture nor in a holding tank awaiting assimilation. Rather, they are participating in the dynamic process of adapting their changing lives to an old culture and a new one – both of which are also changing. The immigrant's journey is one of the mind and the soul, not merely of the body. As they adapt, they develop not only their individual biographical maps but also the history and culture of Toronto.

And so they come – seventy thousand or so every year, bringing their dreams and conceiving their maps; keeping what they cherish of the old ways, and changing, adjusting and contributing to the new, according to their own circumstances, in their own time. Their gathering has been of incalculable benefit to Toronto. It has developed, in our own civic culture, an instinct for respecting individual and group differences that has extended freedom for us all. And, in a city of infinite human diversity, this has given us an extraordinary legacy of social peace.

TORONTO – THE CELEBRATION

TORONTO – THE CELEBRATION

TORONTO – THE CELEBRATION

TORONTO – THE CELEBRATION

TORONTO – THE CELEBRATION

TORONTO – THE CELEBRATION

TORONTO – THE CELEBRATION

TORONTO – THE CELEBRATION

TORONTO – THE CELEBRATION

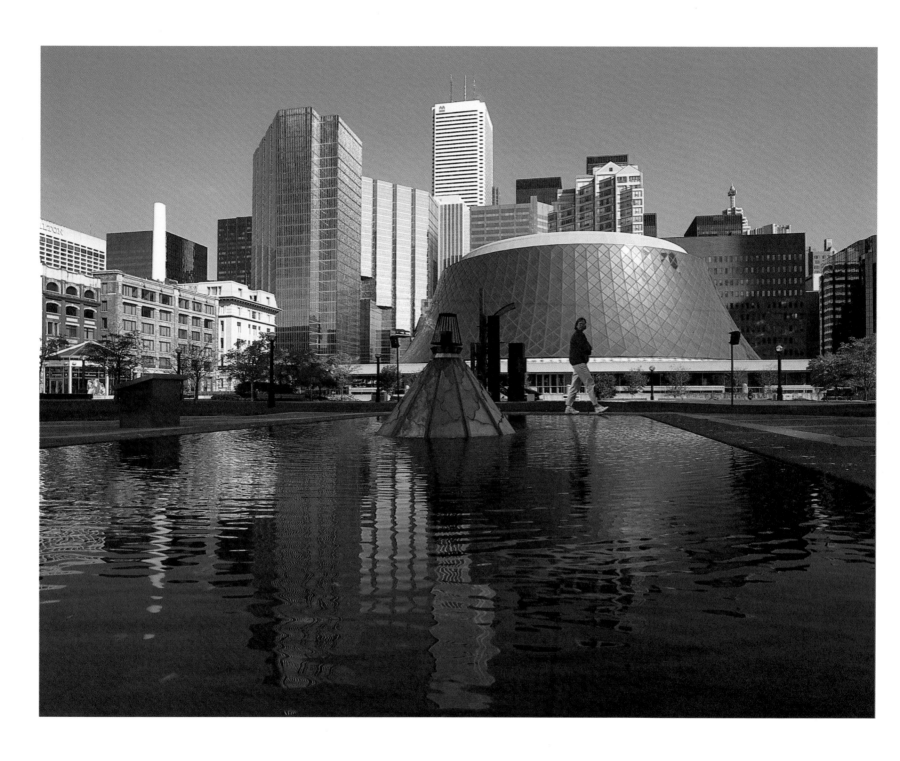

TORONTO – THE CELEBRATION

TORONTO – THE CELEBRATION

A WATERFRONT WORLD

Waterfronts are special places, essential to human development as centres of commerce, and points of arrival and departure. As places to build cities the practical advantage is obvious – water: for drinking, cooking, and cleansing; for transportation and agriculture; but there is more. For the waterfront is a world both real and imagined.

Where nature meets culture, according to ecologist Peter Timmerman, "an energy transfer takes place and, therefore, can be tapped as an energy source; that is why people have settled on the water's edge since the beginning of history."

Toronto was born on the waterfront. Deep in aboriginal time, the Toronto Carrying Place was a centre of trade, stabilized by community and endowed with spiritual significance. When the railways came to Toronto, they literally changed its face: land access to the bay, which had been so vital, diminished in importance. The city cut itself off from its waterfront, allowing dozens of sets of tracks to flow in and out of one another in the new lands south of Front Street.

"Toronto became a magnet for the world's creative people, people with dreams and ideas, people seeking freedom and better prospects, people whose descendants would ensure Toronto's vitality."

Much was lost, but much was gained: the new technology drew hundreds of industries to Toronto over the years, establishing a formula for economic success that is potent to this day. Prosperity meant industry, and industry meant the railways. Like other energetic cities, Toronto became a magnet for the world's creative people, people with dreams and ideas, people seeking freedom and better prospects, people whose descendants would ensure Toronto's vitality. As the industrial base prosperously expanded, however, our concept of nature changed dramatically. The natural significance of waterfronts was slowly lost; the contribution of our river valleys and watersheds was no longer understood or taught, and the essential role of nature in the city was all but forgotten.

"Torontonians now look to the waterfront for pleasure and solace in a way their great-grandparents would have recognized and appreciated."

For a very long time, in the pursuit of needs and pleasures, our throw-away society poisoned the air, polluted the rivers, and contaminated the earth, with neither care nor curiosity about the long-term damage to both the environment and the opportunities of future generations. Unswimmable, undrinkable, and unfishable water became the touchstone of our environmental carelessness.

When we assumed that progress meant degrading our natural and built heritage, we wiped out collective memories. Then, when the winds of change blew, we often felt too shallowly rooted to know what was important to our sense of ourselves. There was a risk that our places would become indistinguishable from others in North America, and that people – even those who had lived in Toronto all their lives – would find themselves increasingly disconnected from it.

But times have changed, and continue to change. Just as the arrival of the railways transformed the city and its waterfront, so their departure is transforming it again; our economic base is changing significantly; and we are responding to new priorities and values. Torontonians now look to the waterfront for pleasure and solace in a way their great-grandparents would have recognized and appreciated.

This dramatic re-connection of waterfront to city is not unique to Toronto. In cities around the world projects are again anchoring their cities to their waterfronts; and, in the process, the meaning of the waterfront is rediscovered.

We are learning that humans are part of the waterfront ecology, not separate from it. Because everything is connected to everything else, we are responsible for our actions – to ourselves, to other people, to other generations, and to other species. As such, we play a large part in the regeneration of the waterfront's ecology, economy and communities. The old practice of moving in, using up, throwing away, and moving on is no longer acceptable.

In "Little Gidding," T. S. Eliot wrote:

> We shall not cease from exploration
> And the end of all our exploring
> Will be to arrive where we started
> And know the place for the first time.

Nowhere is this truer than on the waterfront. We have gone back to fundamentals, to basic principles and essential questions. What purposes should our reclaimed waterfront serve? What should it look like? What should it become – a place to live? A place to work? A place to play? A combination of all of these? Two of them? In what ratios? What proportion? What scale? What kind of work? What kind of play?

In answering these questions, cities define themselves, become different from one another, and develop their specific character. As products of time, place, and circumstance, they become what they are through their treatment by successive generations.

Like people, a city is not separate from nature. In Toronto, we have vegetation, forests, fields, streams, lakes, rivers, soil, and wildlife. Only by recognizing the city as part of nature, can we heal the harm inflicted on it, mend our ways, and ensure that it functions sustainably, to satisfy present needs without diminishing future opportunities.

The ongoing development of the Trail and greenway along Toronto's waterfront and around Lake Ontario is a magnificent testimony to that recognition. The Waterfront Trail stretches some 350 kilometres through 28 municipalities, from Kingston to Niagara; it links 177 natural areas, 143 parks and promenades, hundreds of historic sites, scores of fairs, museums, art galleries and countless communities, neighbourhoods, and industrial areas. It connects inland watersheds to the waterfront through more than 65 rivers and creeks, to their headwaters in the slopes of Oak Ridges Moraine to the north, the Niagara Escarpment and the Bruce Trail to the west.

These life-giving connections form a vast triangular "green net" around Toronto, which influences the urban form of the region, and shapes its biodiversity and environmental health. Trail construction; erosion and sediment control; wildlife preservation; habitat restoration; gardens; park creation and enhancement; children's playgrounds; boat launch facilities; docks; jetties; boardwalks and bridges; community museums; and open-air concert stages are being developed, by a unique network of municipalities, conservation authorities, governments, community groups, foundations, corporations, volunteers, small businesses, and the Waterfront Regeneration Trust. So successful is this undertaking that more and more communities are participating in the Trail's development: it now has the potential to stretch more than 650 kilometres.

The Trail teaches us to understand and appreciate the natural and cultural heritage of the Toronto region. It represents a catalogue of what we have, what we can recycle and reuse, what we must develop, and how we can weave the new into the old. The Trail reminds us of the mutuality of landscapes: natural landscapes, born of ecological processes, meeting our need for environ-mental balance; working rural landscapes, in which goods are produced to feed us and future generations; and city landscapes, which remind us of our cultural heritage and a way of life that embraces us all.

TORONTO – THE CELEBRATION

TORONTO – THE CELEBRATION

TORONTO – THE CELEBRATION

TORONTO – THE CELEBRATION

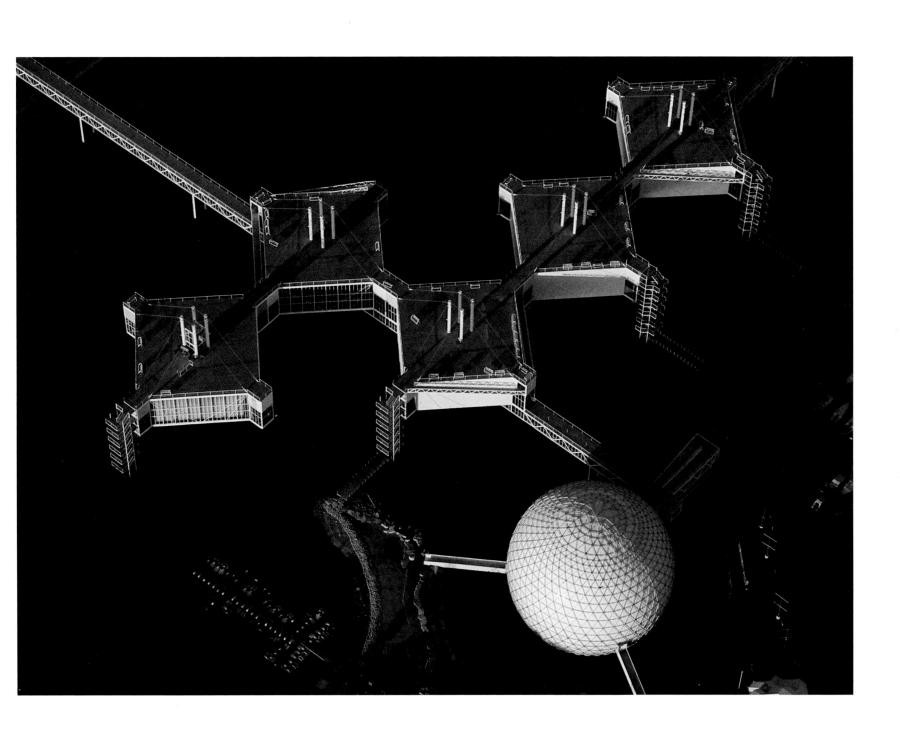

TORONTO – THE CELEBRATION

TORONTO – THE CELEBRATION

The sign reads: WISHING ♥PAPA♥ A HAPPY ★65TH★ ♥BIRTHDAY♥ SURPRISEFROMJACK

TORONTO – THE CELEBRATION

TORONTO – THE CELEBRATION

TORONTO – THE CELEBRATION

TORONTO – THE CELEBRATION

CITY BUILDING

Historically, in North America, the very idea of 'the city' has often been a negative one. Thomas Jefferson regarded the growth of American cities as "pestilential to our future," and much of American literature and social comment reinforces that imagery. Our daily news usually features city crime, violence, drugs, poverty, mendacity, and indifference.

Cities have been criticized as crowded, unhealthy, fearful, vice-ridden, ugly places that spawn plagues and epidemics; Sodoms, where taboos can be broken, moral instruction ignored, and where foreigners with strange ideas and customs corrupt the unwary.

Cities housed Blake's "dark satanic mills," exploited Marx's impoverished urban proletariat, and condemned them to Dickens's tenemented squalor. In our own time, North American cities have been declared unfixable, crime-infested, race-ridden, financial and environmental disasters to be avoided in favour of bucolic towns, suburban enclaves, and rural landscapes.

Simply put, the city is a bad place where bad things happen; the country-side is a good place where good things happen, where people are more human and God more knowable.

While the city-bashers have held sway, cities have not been without their defenders: throughout history and around the world, great works of architecture, vast schemes of city-building, and triumphs of literary imagination have celebrated the city as a temple to the power, wealth, ideology or spirituality of dynasties, empires, and civilizations. The City of God, the City on a Hill, the Holy City, the Garden City, the City Beautiful, the Radiant City – all evoke the divine possibilities of cities, which Lewis Mumford saw as places in which "the separate beams of life" and the "issues of civilization" are brought into focus.

The "city bad, countryside good" attitude may explain, in part, why Canada has always been promoted as a place of pristine mountains, mighty rivers, and empty spaces. Since 1921, however, 80 per cent of all Canadians have lived in cities – most in large metropolitan regions.

Toronto is usually described as clean, safe and livable. It is seen as having learned the secret of maintaining a vital, healthy downtown core in the face of suburban expansion, and as having absorbed waves of multiracial, multicultural migration without succumbing to the pox of racism and the deadening grip of a permanent economic and social underclass. One factor that should never be underestimated in that development is the place of the city in Canadian history.

Canada took shape largely through the exploitation of such staples and resources as fish, fur, forestry, wheat, and precious metals, organized and controlled by imperially supported companies, organizations, and governments linked to large metropolitan centres, domestic and foreign. Indeed, most Canadian cities owe their beginnings and their growth more to trade, commerce, transportation, and government and military establishments than to agriculture and agrarian settlement.

Metropolitan-based forces built regional identities, in a unique counterpoint to the imperial power and, later, to federal and provincial governments. The city – particularly Toronto – was the core of a communications system carrying goods, people, ideas, orders, and money. Everything was connected to everything else through the city.

Thus it became the primary site for inculcating the constitutional values of "peace, order, and good government." By connecting the regional frontier to the power of the metropolitan centre, these values provided a coherent, interdependent context for communities from wilderness to the most rural to the most urban. All people were understood to be part of the whole; and this engendered an appreciation of community, social order, and public behaviour that still informs the standards and expectations of life in Toronto today.

This helped develop a strong sense of loyalty and obedience to law and civil authority. It also legitimized the educational, intellectual, cultural, and moral styles, trends, and standards of the day, mostly dedicated to the personal virtues of industriousness, responsibility, and respect for property. All are still essential to the character of Toronto.

"...there has been a remarkable persistence in Toronto's civic traditions: the 'us' has proven, generally speaking, stronger than the 'me' or the 'them'."

While some of this sturdy public morality has, perhaps, eroded, there has been a remarkable persistence in Toronto's civic traditions: the "us" has proven, generally speaking, stronger than the "me" or the "them." One need only look at our responses to such public issues as public order, gun control, and public health to see how, over time, small, incremental, step-by-step willingness to change pays substantial dividends of social peace.

Learning how to keep public order in an increasingly multicultural Toronto has meant redrawing and redefining the limits of public order and public behaviour, so the customs and habits of "newcomers" would be served, while order was maintained. None of this has involved legislation, but it has meant that everyone — especially politicians, the police, and the media — have had to learn how different communities organize themselves, and to recognize and respect differences. Such efforts, in these and other matters, have been plain common sense in Toronto: if we are going to maintain anything close to our traditional belief in public order, it cannot be on the basis of "us" and "them". Only through co-habitation can the imperative for peace and order be fulfilled.

This is both the reason for and the result of a marked difference in the role of the gun in American and Canadian society. The difference flows from divergent assumptions toward public authority.

In Canada it was the Crown and its officers, not individuals, who were charged with the responsibility of maintaining and ensuring individual rights in the context of the community's peace and order. Indeed, many Canadian cities were founded as military posts and bastions of the Empire. Peace and order on the "frontier" were ensured not by individual fire power but by officers representing the Queen's law. The peaceful use of guns by farmers, hunters, sports enthusiasts, and others, was, of course, lawful; but such privilege was never confused with the "right" to use a gun against other human beings. Who could bear arms and who had the right to command behaviour by the use of force was a Crown monopoly.

The primacy of "us" over "me" or "them," which strongly affects the livability of life in Toronto can also be found in such Canadian expressions of common good as universal health care. Like education, the right to health care is seen as fundamental to equality of opportunity: people should not be expected to suffer and die because they cannot afford the costs of care, any more than personal finances should decide who is educated and who is not.

Toronto has benefited from the contribution that publicly funded health-care makes to equality of opportunity: the ability of diverse people to live harmoniously with one another is powerfully supported by public expenditures on one's personal health, and by the resulting sense that the system really works — and that it works for each of us.

Moreover, Toronto experience shows that a solid, stable health-care system leads to thinking about health in broader terms, and that it can significantly influence public policy making. Environmental and planning issues are increasingly being articulated through the prism of individual health. For example, smoking has now been banished from the workplace and the marketplace, from stores, and from virtually all public places where people congregate.

In the past few years, Toronto has expanded to include within its orbit cities, towns, villages, farms, forests, wetlands, rivers and valleys, home to almost five million people. This vast, multi-connected place spans scores of kilometres and links people to places and spaces where they live, work and play, bound together by a web of roads, highways, rail lines, jetports, telephones, radios, computers, faxes, satellites, televisions and "smart" buildings. The city of stable neighbourhoods and the sturdy downtown that has gathered people from all over the globe has become an extraordinary centre of communications that links Toronto to the world.

"The city of stable neighbourhoods and the sturdy downtown that has gathered people from all over the globe has become an extraordinary centre of communications that links Toronto to the world."

It has also become a site of extraordinary change, as human migration and technological revolution, ecological imperatives, and new global perspectives combine to expand its future significantly. These forces of transformation herald new values; overwhelm traditional, local jurisdictions; and push aside old boundaries and borders. In response, governments are rethinking policies and programs; corporations are reassessing strategies and priorities; and community and individual responsibilities are being redefined.

It is in the communities, neighbourhoods, and workplaces of Toronto where change is taking place and real people are being affected. Here jobs are lost, new skills developed, and careers pursued. Here values and ideas are recast. Here hope and fear contend, as individuals, races, ethnicities, languages, cultures, and social groups jostle for a place in the new order.

In the process, people change, and make change. They change not only the physical appearance of the city, suburb and countryside, but the nature of the workplace, patterns of leisure, politics, art, music, and public tastes and manners. Walk down any busy street, visit parks, playgrounds, workplaces, malls, restaurants, cafés, hockey rinks, waterfronts, wedding halls, subways, and places of worship — any site where people congregate — and you will see and feel the change.

How do we take stock of these extraordinary changes? How do we take account of this historic movement of people? How do we benefit from technological and economic revolutions, and deal with the environmental imperatives that need our attention?

In *Making Democracy Work*, Robert Putnam emphasizes the crucial importance of understanding the traditions of one's own civic culture, particularly in times of significant change. Of course, the culture of any particular city differs from that of any other. As political and social entities, cities are shaped by their particular histories, laws, customs, founding moments, and challenges.

Moreover, there is no perfect city. Inevitably our generation's changes will be changed, in turn, by those who come after us; but we know that change comes as a better friend when it enters a context of continuity and community.

A city's particular history and culture matter because they allow one to understand the place better and, therefore, to identify what must be done to repair, regenerate, and sustain it. At the core of Toronto's civic culture lie some essential organizing ideas that have served it well.

First, people must be free to pursue their material interests, to their benefit, and to that of their family and community. This is not glib, but the expression of a deep and universal human need. People come to a place and are willing to stay because that place holds better prospects. That is why Toronto has always tried to maintain local economic strength in the face of increasingly global competition.

Second, Toronto is rediscovering a venerable truth: economic strength, environmental health, and social well-being are not mutually exclusive. They are, in fact, interdependent. This connectedness demands that we plan and accept with an eye to the effects our actions have on ourselves, the future and the biosphere. To do otherwise is not only morally indefensible but economically destructive.

> *"Toronto has always acted best when it remembered the historic promise of cities."*

Third, Torontonians have always understood the importance to people of place and community, as the physical and psychic spaces in which human personalities are formed and expressed; in which identities are learned and re-learned; and in which the rudiments of survival are gleaned and practised. Here are early and continuing responses to such fundamental questions as Who am I? What do I believe? How do I behave? Where do I belong?

Fourth, in the new century, personal security and public order will be highly prized in cities around the world. Toronto has always understood that such assets are accrued only through a social peace which is achieved not merely by the absence of conflict but flows from the increasing presence of justice and equity for its citizens, and the willingness, both privately and publicly, to foster a culture of caring.

Finally, Toronto has always acted best when it remembered the historic promise of cities. Human beings, as Jane Jacobs points out, "are the only city-building creatures in the world…Whenever and wherever societies have flourished and prospered… cities have been at the core of the phenomenon".

For centuries, people have gone down the road to the cities of the world. Cities have been places of opportunity, where they can build, change and transform. In cities, the real mingles with the imagined — you can try to be what you want to be. There, if you're lucky, you find a sense of community that meets your needs, shapes your day-to-day experiences, gives focus to your freedom and meaning to your hopes. If the new century brings all that to you, then you will have every reason to celebrate Toronto.

TORONTO – THE CELEBRATION

TORONTO – THE CELEBRATION

TORONTO – THE CELEBRATION

TORONTO – THE CELEBRATION

TORONTO – THE CELEBRATION

TORONTO – THE CELEBRATION

TORONTO – THE CELEBRATION

TORONTO – THE CELEBRATION

TORONTO – THE CELEBRATION

174

TORONTO – THE CELEBRATION

PHOTOGRAPHS

13   *Since 1976, the CN Tower has ranked as the world's tallest freestanding tourist magnet at 1,815 feet (553.33 metres) from the ground to its lightening rod tip. While most visitors prefer the elevator, the tower's 1,776 steps provide a challenging course for competitors in various charity fund-raising stair climbs.*

14   *Sunrise on the twin towers of BCE Place in the city's business centre.*

16   *The magnificent five-storey arch of steel, granite and glass links the two towers of BCE Place. At left, the Commercial Bank of the Midland District, designed by architect William Thomas in the 1840s. It was disassembled and moved here from its original home on Wellington Street in the early 1990s.*

17   *Early skyscrapers at King and Yonge Streets stand as reminders of the old metropolis.*

18   *The richly coffered gold-leafed ceiling of the 1929 Bank of Commerce building casts a greenish glow over the immense main hall of the building.*

19   *Easy riders on Yonge Street at Adelaide.*

20   *On location at Temperance Street in "Hollywood North".*

21   *Chefs take a break in the courtyard of Biagio's restaurant, King and Jarvis.*

22   *Street eats and satisfied customers at Union Station.*

23   *Moving through time…from Union Station across its clock tower to one of the golden towers of the Royal Bank Plaza. A grand monument of the twenties, Union Station formally opened in 1927 and still ranks first among Canada's railway stations for sheer size and magnificence. Built in 1976, the Royal Bank Plaza, with its shimmering serrated gold exterior, seems as much sculpture as architecture.*

24   *Another business day winds down at the Toronto-Dominion Centre. Designed by Mies van der Rohe, its starkly elegant black steel-and-glass towers embody 1960s modern architecture.*

25   *A patch of blue caps the urban sculpture of Toronto's bank towers.*

26   *"New" City Hall, a modernist masterpiece designed by Viljo Revell of Finland, winner of an international competition. Since opening in 1965, to Toronto's municipal administration – and mixed reviews – it still holds its own as a Toronto landmark.*

27   *The Toronto Annual Outdoor Art Exhibition takes over the vast concrete canvas of Nathan Phillips Square on the second weekend in July.*

28   *The grand staircase at Osgoode Hall, one of the most elegant historic buildings still left in this city. The headquarters of the Law Society of Upper Canada since the 1830s, this aristocratic structure is also home to Ontario's Supreme Court.*

29   *Radiant skylight in the upper rotunda of Osgoode Hall.*

30   *Hart House, with its late-Gothic Oxbridge tower, sits serenely on the sprawling St. George campus of the University of Toronto. Donated by the Massey Foundation in 1919, Hart House serves as a student union for recreation and the arts. Its Great Hall is the social hub of the university.*

31   *Late afternoon studies on the St. George campus.*

32   *The Hart House quadrangle.*

33   *Spring blooms on the terrace of Trinity College, built Gothic-style in 1925. The lovely chapel was added in the 1950s and is one of the most admired buildings on campus.*

34   *Dinosaur Gallery at the Royal Ontario Museum. Opened in 1912, the ROM remains Canada's largest public museum.*

35   *Contrasting architectural styles of the Hydro Building, Queen's Park and Whitney Block.*

36   *War memorial in Queen's Park.*

37   *An oasis of peace on the Queen's Park grounds.*

38   *Fall foliage camouflages the rooftops of Rosedale, the greenest neighbourhood in the heart of the city.*

39   *A misty morning at the Prince Edward Viaduct (commonly referred to as the Bloor-Danforth Viaduct). Designed by architect Edmund Burke, and completed in 1919, its massive concrete pylons and hinged steel arches span the Don Valley.*

40   *The Bain Co-op, originally known as Riverdale Court, was one of Toronto's first public housing experiments around the turn of the century.*

41   *The Bloor-Danforth Viaduct looking north to highrises on Overlea Boulevard.*

42   *Parade in "Greektown" on the Danforth.*

43   *"Taste of the Danforth" annual food festival.*

44   *"Little India", a bustling stretch of clothing stores, spice shops and restaurants strung along six blocks on Gerrard Street East.*

The Beaches

Settled as a summer place in the 1880s, The Beach, as locals prefer to call it, was Toronto's earliest "cottage country." Some of its New England charm is still evident in the numerous clapboard style homes.

45   *Morning fog settles on The Beach.*

46   *Musician serenades strollers on the boardwalk.*

47   *The Easter Parade makes its way along Queen Street East.*

48   *Kayaker in the early morning solitude of The Beach.*

49   *The R.C. Harris Filtration Plant – a fine example of "engineering raised to an art." Built Art Deco style in the early thirties, the plant was part of a much needed and major improvement in the city's water supply.*

58   *The Scarborough Bluffs, a spectacular natural sculpture rising 200 feet and stretching 9 miles along the lakeshore. Evident in its layers are five glacial ages and prehistoric lakes. Unfortunately, the Bluffs are subject to on-going erosion.*

60   *Wedding amongst the ruins at the Guild Inn. Founded in 1932 as an artist's colony by Spencer Clark and his wife, the inn is home to a gloriously eccentric collection of bits and pieces of Toronto's demolished old buildings. These architectural fragments, collected in the 60s and 70s, are scattered among the flowerbeds and hedges perched on the crest of the Scarborough Bluffs.*

61   *Scarborough Civic Centre, acclaimed for its superb architecture by Ray Moriyama. Designed in the early seventies, its five-storey public arena and lively square create a focal point in the sprawling Scarborough landscape.*

62   *The Metropolitan Toronto Zoo, where this nosy giraffe and about 5,000 other creatures make their home on the 700-acre Rouge Hill site.*

63   *Edwards Gardens, one of Toronto's first garden parks. The land, originally settled in 1817, was, after a series of owners, sold to Metro Toronto Parks in 1956. It's been a mecca for wedding photographers ever since.*

64   *The Novotel Hotel, a visually striking component of North York City Centre, was designed by Moriyama & Teshima Architects and built in 1987.*

65   *The Winter Garden Theatre, together with the Elgin Theatre, form one of the world's last remaining double-decker theatre complexes. Opened as an "atmospheric theatre" to vaudeville audiences in 1914, the Winter Garden closed in 1928, while the lower Elgin auditorium continued for a time as a movie theatre. After being declared a national historic site, the complex was fully restored by The Ontario Heritage Foundation for live theatre. Its grand re-opening took place in 1989.*

66   *Fearless rock climber at the Toronto Street Festival on Yonge Street.*

67   *Yonge Street, more midway than main street, especially at Dundas, where*
      Sam the Record Man remains a landmark. Yonge Street "the longest street
      in the world" stretches 1,900 kilometres to the west of Lake Superior.

68   *Filmores Hotel on Dundas Street East, offering "adult entertainment" since the sixties.*

69   *The Village of Yorkville Park, with its high-tech architectural structures, induced mist*
      and twinkling lights, centres around a 650-tonne granite rock. This massive boulder
      was sawed into 135 pieces, then transported from the Muskokas and reassembled.
      The park's intriguing design is the result of a 1991 international competition won
      by Oleson Worland Architects.

70   *Man in red by high-tech fountain, Village of Yorkville Park.*

71   *Puttin' on the ritz – Cumberland Street in Yorkville.*

72   *Mirvish Village – with its galleries, craft studios and bookshops, is as colourful as its*
      creator, Ed Mirvish.

73   *Street performer amuses crowd in the Annex area. Nearby, Ye Olde Brunswick House,*
      built in 1876, is still a popular neighbourhood watering hole.

74   *Casa Loma, grandiose creation of eccentric financier Sir Henry Pellatt, who clearly*
      lived by the adage "A man's home is his castle." Designed by E.J. Lennox, also the
      architect of Old City Hall, it was completed in 1914 and boasts 98 rooms,
      21 fireplaces and numerous secret passageways. Casa Loma was converted to
      a tourist attraction in 1937, after a turn of fortune forced Pellatt to leave.

75   *Motorcyclists take a break outside the Café Diplomatico, a favourite of people-*
      watchers since 1968, long before College Street West became a hip strip.

76   *Grand circular staircase at the Grange, one of Toronto's first brick buildings.*
      Built for the wealthy Boulton family in 1817, it later became the first home of
      the Art Gallery, which housed its offices there until the seventies, when it was fully
      restored and opened to the public. The rear façade of this elegant Georgian-style
      home was later integrated with the Art Gallery of Ontario's sculpture gallery.

77   *Costumed interpreter from the Grange steps briefly out of the 19th century to admire*
      a sculpture in the adjacent Tannenbaum Sculpture Atrium, Art Gallery of Ontario.

78   *Caught up in the excitement of World Cup Soccer celebrations in Little Italy,*
      College Street West.

79   *Kensington Market, one of Canada's last open-air markets, was once the heart of Jewish*
      Toronto in the early 1900s. It's grown into a lively multi-cultural bazaar – streets
      brimming with import and grocery stores, vintage clothing shops, cafés and nightclubs.

80   *Lamps for sale! Kensington Market area.*

81   *The SkyDome has landed! Looking south along Spadina Avenue.*

82   *The largest of Toronto's Chinatowns teems with vendors and shoppers along Spadina Avenue.*

Queen Street West

83   *The Black Bull Tavern on Queen Street West, began as an inn back in 1833 and has become a favourite with the biker crowd.*

84   *Treasures abound in Queen West's numerous secondhand shops.*

85   *Squeegee kids strike a pose.*

86   *The Theatre District is home to the venerable Royal Alexandra – built in 1907, then rescued and restored in the sixties – and the Princess of Wales Theatre, built in 1994. Several restaurants and an antique shop complete this part of the Mirvish Walkway on King Street West.*

87   *The CityTV truck (the collaborative effort of four company executives), adorns the 1915 Wesley Building, home to the ChumCity broadcast empire since the mid-eighties.*

88   *Queen West, a place to see and be seen.*

89   *Custom car-detailing turns a few heads.*

90   *Walking on water – Roy Thomson Hall, home to the Toronto Symphony and the Mendelssohn Choir since 1982. Its dazzling 40,000-square-foot mirrored glass exterior was designed by Canadian architect Arthur Erickson.*

91   *The SkyDome, home of the Blue Jays and the Argonauts. Built in 1989, with the world's first fully-retractable stadium roof, SkyDome boosted the city's reputation into the urban major leagues.*

92   *Michael Snow's whimsical sculptures greet fans at the SkyDome entrance.*

93   *The Air Canada Centre, home to the Maple Leafs and the Raptors since February 1999, when Toronto witnessed the end of a legendary era at Maple Leaf Gardens. Here, the Leafs play the visiting St. Louis Blues in the inaugural season.*

94   *Toronto Molson Indy Circuit at Exhibition Place – a roaring success since it began in 1986.*

95   *The National Trade Centre at Exhibition Place. Completed in 1997, its sleek glass front and dramatic tower beacons put a fresh face on the 19th century exhibition grounds. Designed by Zeidler Roberts/Dunlop Farrow Inc.*

102   *The Caribana Parade, highlight of the city's largest cultural festival, heats up the streets at the end of July and early August.*

103   *The construction of Caribana's elaborate parade floats and costumes has grown into a local art form and industry.*

104   *Simcoe Park sculpture "untitled mountain", by Anish Kapoor, 1995. Part of the collection of public art gracing Simcoe Place. This site once housed the seat of Parliament of Upper Canada from 1829 to 1841.*

105   *City view from the Bathurst Bridge, south of Front Street.*

106   *Built in 1783 by Governor John Graves Simcoe, Fort York was destroyed by American troops in 1813 and restored soon afterward for the use of Canadian military. After extensive renovations in the 1930s, it was converted into a thriving tourist attraction. Later, it survived an entirely different kind of battle – that with Metro Councillors wanting to move it out of the path of the Gardiner Expressway. It remains the oldest continuously maintained fort in Canada.*

107   *Going for a spin on the Midway at the Canadian National Exhibition – an end-of-summer ritual for generations since 1878.*

108   *Ontario Place, designed by Eberhard Zeidler opened in 1971, as a "creative leisure time space available to all."*

109   *Ontario Place, one of the most architecturally distinctive landmarks on the lakeshore.*

110   *Skyline at dusk.*

111   *Grenadier Pond in High Park.*

112   *The Humber River Bicycle-Pedestrian Bridge, completed in 1996, has become an instant landmark along Lake Ontario's shoreline, as well as an integral part of the waterfront trail system. Its award-winning design by Montgomery and Sisam Architects incorporates historical and aboriginal motifs.*

113   *View from the Mimico Cruising Club towards the Marina Del Rey condominiums along Lake Shore Boulevard, Etobicoke.*

114   *The Cruise Motel stands as part of a bygone era on the Motel Strip in Etobicoke. Though its glory days have passed, this section of Lake Shore Boulevard has its own charms and historical significance.*

115   *Home sweet home, Etobicoke.*

116   *Salmon fishing on the Humber River, just north of Bloor Street.*

117   *Site of the King's Mill, built on the banks of the Humber River in 1793, to process lumber for the proposed town of York. A series of fires forced it to be rebuilt three times. Today, the remaining walls of the last grist mill, destroyed in 1881, grace the grounds behind The Old Mill restaurant.*

Black Creek Pioneer Village

A collection of period buildings added to the original farm of Daniel Stong, evoking 19th century life in rural Ontario.

118   *Cyclist without benefit of gear shift.*

119   *Going for the biggest piece of the pie.*

120   *19th century-style jam session.*

121   *Woodbine Race Track, where the "Sport of Kings" enjoys the largest racing property in North America. Racing events include the venerable Queen's Plate, Canadian International, North America Cup and the Canadian Pacing Derby.*

122   *Morning skyline over Riverdale Park.*

123   *Participants strut their stuff in the Gay Pride Parade, an annual event since 1981.*

124   *Coming out for the fun of it at the Gay Pride Parade.*

125   *Cabbagetown, originally settled by British and Irish immigrants in the mid 1800s, was predominately a working class neighbourhood. It has, for the most part, been gentrified and now symbolizes affluent downtown living.*

126   *The Necropolis Chapel in Cabbagetown. Built in 1872, its slate roof, tracery and ironwork have been beautifully preserved. The chapel remains one of the finest examples of High Victorian Gothic architecture.*

127   *The Necropolis, one of Toronto's oldest non-sectarian burial grounds, dates from the early 1850s. It is the final resting place of William Lyon Mackenzie, Toronto's first mayor and leader of the Rebellion of 1837.*

128   *A mural decorates the wall of the Danny Grossman Dance Company in Cabbagetown.*

129   *The Wellesley Cottages in Cabbagetown, once modest working-class dwellings at the turn of the century. Though modernized, this row of simple gabled cottages retains its charm.*

130   *Scrutinizing a human scarecrow at Riverdale Farm.*

131   *Bright Street, on Toronto's east side. Originally built as worker's housing before the turn of the century, these little rowhouses appear to tilt closer towards the curb with every passing year.*

132   *Serving up Jamaican fare, The Real Jerk brightens the corner of Queen and Broadview.*

133   *The Canary Grill has been run by the same family since the mid-seventies. This retro diner is a Toronto landmark and a favourite location for film makers. Built in the late 1850s as a public school, it was later converted to a small hotel and now houses several small businesses.*

134   *The Docks, accessible by boat, car…or blades.*

135   *The Docks, a 21-acre entertainment complex on the lakefront off Cherry Street, boasts "Canada's largest patio."*

136   *The mural, "hunter" by Wyland, adorns the north side of the Redpath sugar refinery, built on the lakefront in 1959.*

137   *The waterfront, home to upscale condominiums, hotels and cultural hub Harbourfront Centre, was a rundown assortment of factories, warehouses and docks until the early seventies, when the 100-acre site was completely renovated.*

148   *In the icy grip of winter, on Clarke Beach.*

149   *Coach house in Rosedale, Toronto's oldest surviving residential "suburb". This affluent area had its beginnings in the early 1800s, as the estate of Sheriff William Jarvis and his wife Mary, who named it after the wild roses blooming around their house.*

150   *Ships retired for the season.*

152   *Harbour sunset.*

153   *Lamp transformed to sculpture.*

154   *Skating in Riverdale Park, a favourite pastime since the turn of the century.*

155 *Todmorden Mills, an open-air museum nestled in the Don Valley, contains two restored Confederation houses, a paper mill, a former brewery and the old Don railway station.*

156 *The Santa Claus Parade, a century-old tradition, proceeding south from Bloor down Avenue Road.*

157 *The party's over and costumes are shed as the Santa Claus Parade winds down on Berkeley Street.*

158 *At the pull of a switch, over 100,000 lights are turned on, as the annual Festival of Lights kicks off the winter season in Nathan Phillips Square.*

159 *Skaters on melting ice, Nathan Phillips Square.*

160 *Skating on Grenadier Pond, so-named for British soldiers who used the frozen surface in High Park for drills and exercises in the 1830s.*

161 *Skaters enjoy "Canada's largest outdoor artificial rink" at Harbourfront Centre.*

162 *St. James' Cathedral, Toronto's first Anglican cathedral, and St. James Park. Built in 1850, the cathedral is the fourth St. James on the site, built on the ruins of its predecessor, which burned in the Great Fire of 1849.*

163 *St. James' Park, dormant until spring, when it is transformed into a lovely 19th century garden.*

The Toronto Islands

164 *Pushing through icy waters, this ferry serves Ward's and Algonquin Island residents during the winter season, as well as visitors in the summer.*

165 *Dedicated news buffs share a bench in Toronto Island Park.*

166 *Creative tableau on veranda of Ward's Island cottage.*

167 *Home sweet home, Ward's Island. Though the Islands have been host to a residential community since the 1800s, most of the cottages on Ward's date from the 1930s.*

168 *Boats linger in one of the Island's many lagoons.*

169 *Skyline overview of the Toronto Islands, with the Leslie Street Spit jutting out from behind.*

170   *Overview of the St. James' Cathedral and the Flatiron Building in the St. Lawrence district. The Gooderhams' Flatiron Building was erected for distillery king and businessman George Gooderham in 1892 on the triangle-shaped lot at Wellington, Front and Church streets. Its trompe l'oeil mural created by Calgary artist Derek Besant in 1980.*

171   *Still visible in the façade of the St. Lawrence Market, are the remains of the original city hall built there in 1844. Converted into a public market in 1904 and later expanded, its lively atmosphere continues to attract shoppers city-wide.*

172   *From its humble beginnings as Muddy York, a world class city comes to light.*

174   *The St. Lawrence Hall, King and Jarvis. Built in lavish Classical style in 1850, this municipal building had been host to gala concerts, formal balls, banquets and public meetings. Among those who appeared there were John A. MacDonald, Jenny Lind, P.T. Barnum's Tom Thumb and Pierre Trudeau. After decades of decline, it was rescued by a public campaign and restored in 1968. It was, for several years, home to the National Ballet of Canada.*

175   *The Gooderham & Worts distillery on Mill Street, originally a flour mill in 1831, saw its profits rise sharply when it turned to distilling spirits. By the 1870s it was producing one-third of all the spirits in Canada. Though several sectors have been transformed and gentrified, this austere Victorian structure remains a Toronto landmark.*

176   *Toronto Sculpture Garden, host to an intriguing variety of installation art since 1981. Exhibits in this small park at King and Church Streets are changed twice a year. Here, 'Greenroom' by artists Millie Chen and Warren Quigley.*

177   *Looking west along historic Front Street, where Toronto's "downtown" had its beginnings.*

178   *Destination: Union Station.*

Photographer's Notes

Rediscovering Toronto through my camera.

It's been more than a few years since my last two books on Toronto were published, though I have been photographing this city off and on since the early seventies.

In spring of 1997 I decided to make a serious attempt at rediscovering Toronto through my camera. Besides purchasing a small bundle of film, I also bought a bicycle – small details are more visible to the cyclist than the driver – and some bungee cords to strap my bag of Leicas on the carrier.

I began with the ever-changing downtown area, explored the Beaches, then widened my focus to other areas of the new City of Toronto – among them Scarborough, North York and Etobicoke. I've enjoyed coffee at the Guild Inn, curry in Little India, a sandwich in Kensington Market, a beer at the Old Mill. Toronto definitely had grown – thank God I was in good shape for cycling.

Two years have gone by, and I'm running out of time for this photo essay. The presses are waiting and the book is going to print. Have I actually finished this project? Not really. There is always another shot to be taken – a new building, another neighbourhood, a fresh perspective of a familiar subject.

The majority of my photographs were done over the past two years – though I did include several older shots – so there may be a small chance that you, dear reader, may find a somewhat younger version of yourself sitting on a park bench or going for a stroll on the boardwalk. I would also like to mention that, despite this age of digital image manipulations, my photographs are not computer-enhanced in any way.

I do hope that this book will inspire you – Torontonian and traveller alike – to rediscover and further explore our remarkable city.

R. Christl

Rudi Christl,
June, 1999.